For The Love Of
READING

· ·

A JOURNAL FOR BOOKAHOLICS

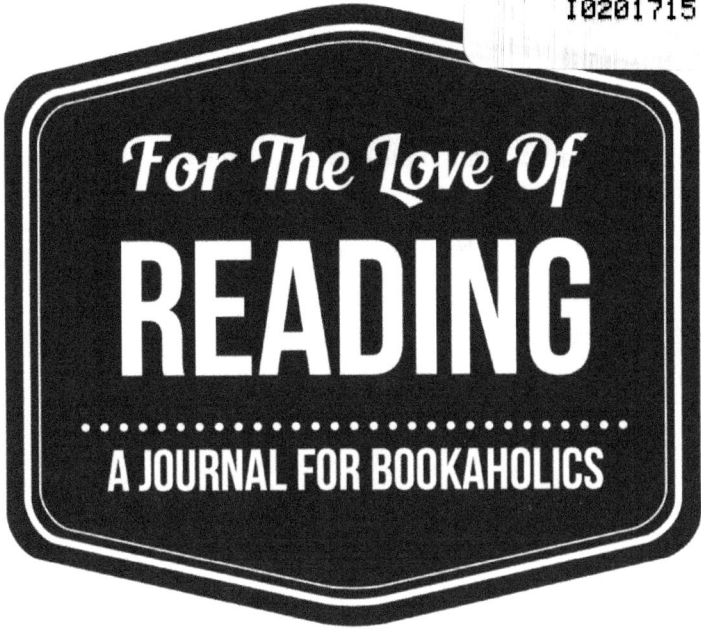

WONDERSTRUCK BOOKS

KANSAS CITY, KS

Dedication

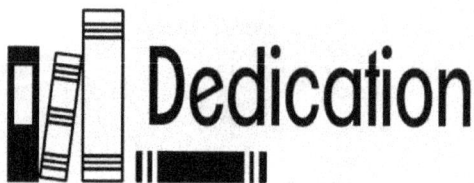

To all the authors who have fed my imagination from childhood through my teen years to today. May your fingers have many more productive hours tapping away on your keyboard!

Published by Wonderstruck Books, Kansas City, KS
ISBN: 978-0998088624
Cover Design by Danyelle Ferguson
Cover Design © 2016 by Danyelle Ferguson
Front cover photography by
Interior Graphic Design credits: TWG Designs, Tyler Warren Graphics, Pretty Grafik Design, Studio Kitsch, Striped Elephants, Miss Tiina
Quote Permissions: Danyelle Ferguson, Lisa Swinton, Carolyn Twede Frank, Project Gutenberg, Loralee Evans

My Book
LIFE

MAR 0 3 2007

MAR 1 4 2007

APR 0 5 2007

MAY 2 2 2007

JUN 0 2 2007

JUN 1 3 2007

JUN 2 1 2007

AUG 0 8 2007

AUG 1 5 2007

AUG 1 7 2007

1

Keep this card in the book pocket—
Book is due on the latest date stamped

2

NO. 314

AUTHOR

TITLE

DATE DUE	BORROWER'S NAME	ROO NUMB.

Books to Read

Books to Read

_____

_____

_____

_____

_____

_____

_____

_____

_____

_____

_____

_____

_____

_____

_____

My Favorite Reading Nooks

My Favorite Bookstores

"The person,
be it a gentleman or lady,
who has not pleasure
in a good novel,

MUST BE
INTOLERABLY STUPID."

- JANE AUSTEN, NORTHANGER ABBEY

LIBRARIES I LOVE

My Favorite Book Blogs & Websites

People I Turn to for Book Recommendations

QUOTES I LOVE

QUOTES I LOVE

If I Had a Time Machine, I'd Travel to . . .

Books Make The Best Gifts

Title/Author   Gifted To

Books Make The Best Gifts

Title/Author   Received From

Amazing Book Covers

Snacks I Munch On While Reading

STORIES I'D LOVE TO WRITE

STORIES I'D LOVE TO WRITE

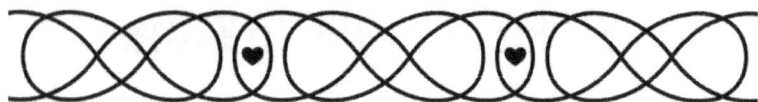

"My world, my world . . .
How can such
a good little girl like you
destroy all
of my beautiful wickedness?"

L. Frank Baum
The Wonderful Wizard of Oz

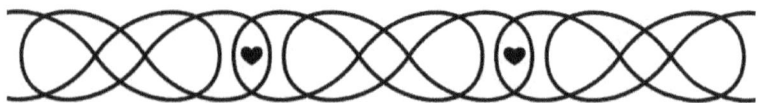

Author

PAGES

AUTHOR

TITLE

DATE DUE	BORROWER'S NAME	ROO NUMB

AUTHORS I LOVE

AUTHORS I  LOVE

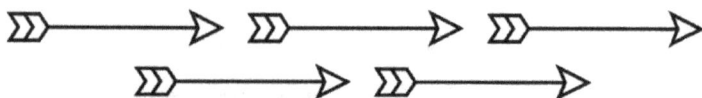

"He who jumps
for the moon
and gets it not
leaps higher
than he who stoops
for a penny in the mud."

Howard Pyle
The Merry Adventures of Robin Hood

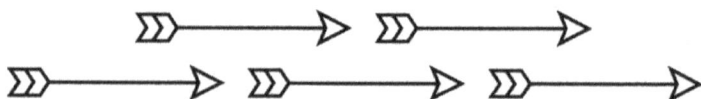

Authors I Follow
on Social Media

_____

_____

_____

_____

_____

_____

_____

_____

_____

_____

_____

_____

_____

_____

Author/Writing
Workshops I've Attended

Authors I've Met

_____

_____

_____

_____

_____

_____

_____

_____

_____

_____

_____

_____

_____

_____

_____

♥—♥—♥—♥—♥—♥—♥—♥—♥—♥

"Grandma always said
to never be afraid
of change because
it could lead to some of
the best things in life.

I sure hope you're right,
Grandma, cause I'm
jumping in-
work boots, tool belt
and all."

Danyelle Ferguson
Love Under Construction

♥—♥—♥—♥—♥—♥—♥—♥—♥—♥

Genre
PAGES

MAR 0 3 2007   AUG 1 7 2007
MAR 1 4 2007
APR 0 5 2007
MAY 2 2 2007
JUN 0 2 2007
JUN 1 3 2007
JUN 2 1 2007
AUG 0 8 2007
AUG 1 5 2007

Keep this card in the book pocket.
Book is due on the latest date stamped.

AUTHOR

TITLE

DATE DUE   BORROWER'S NAME   ROOM NUMBER

No. 314

MY FAVORITE CLASSIC NOVELS

MY FAVORITE HISTORICAL NOVELS

"If ever there is a tomorrow
when we're not together . . .
There is something you

MUST ALWAYS REMEMBER.

you are braver
than you believe

STRONGER
THAN YOU SEEM
and
SMARTER than you think.

But the most important thing is,
even if we're apart . . .

I'll always be with you."

- A. A. MILNE, WINNIE THE POOH

My Favorite
Children's Books

_____

_____

_____

_____

_____

_____

_____

_____

_____

_____

_____

_____

_____

_____

_____

_____

MY FAVORITE SUPER HERO NOVELS

MY FAVORITE DYSTOPIAN NOVELS

▶▶▶▶▶▶▶▶▶▶▶▶▶▶▶

"HOW OFTEN
HAVE I SAID TO YOU
THAT WHEN YOU HAVE
ELIMINATED THE IMPOSSIBLE,
WHATEVER REMAINS,
HOWEVER IMPROBABLE,
MUST BE THE TRUTH?"

SIR ARTHUR CONAN DOYLE
SHERLOCK HOLMES - THE SIGN OF THE FOUR

◀◀◀◀◀◀◀◀◀◀◀◀◀◀◀

MY FAVORITE
SUSPSENSE/MYSTERY BOOKS

SELF-HELP BOOKS
THAT ACTUALLY HELPED

_____

_____

_____

_____

_____

_____

_____

_____

_____

_____

_____

_____

_____

_____

_____

MEMOIRES, AUTOBIOGRAPHIES, AND BIOGRAPHIES I RECOMMEND

My Favorite Holiday Books

My Favorite Sci-Fi Books

The Best Magic and Fantasy Novels

AWESOME STEAMPUNK

CREEPY HORROR NOVELS

"I've got a vocal crush on you.
The first time I heard
you sing I was hooked.
You stole my heart.
It's all yours."

Lisa Swinton
Vocal Crush

My Favorite Romance Novels

>>>>>>>>>>>>>>>>>>>>>>>>>>>>>>>

"We're human;
we're going to make
mistakes. Some of us
are going to learn
and grow
from those mistakes,
and some won't."

Carolyn Twede Frank
Rememberance
Quantum Faith Effect series #3

>>>>>>>>>>>>>>>>>>>>>>>>>>>>>>>

More Book LISTS

AUTHOR

TITLE

DATE DUE	BORROWER'S NAME	ROO NUMB

Books I Read in Elementry School

Books I Read in Middle School

Books I Read in High School

Books I Read in College

"There is nothing
in the world
so irresistibly contagious
as laughter
and good humor."

Charles Dickens
A Christmas Carol

Books That Made Me Laugh

Books That Require
a Box of Tissues

Books That Made Me
Want to Hide Under the Covers

Favorite Book Beginnings

Favorite Book Endings

BOOKS I READ ON VACATION

My Favorite Movies
That Were From Books

Books Made Into
Movies That Were Awful

Books I Wish
Were Made Into Movies

Incredible Audio Books

"But especially he loved
to run in the dim twilight
of the summer midnights,
listening to the subdued
and sleepy murmurs
of the forest,
reading signs and sounds
as a man may read
a book, and seeking
for the mysterious
something that called -
called, waking or sleeping,
at all times,
for him to come."

Jack London
Call of the Wild

Controversial Books I Read

Book Endings That Made Me Scream and Throw the Book Across the Room

----

Books That Were So Not For Me
And I Didn't Finish Them

Character
PAGES

AUTHOR

TITLE

DATE DUE	BORROWER'S NAME	ROOM NUMB

Characters Who Were My Best Friends

Characters Who Annoyed Me

♥—♥—♥—♥—♥—♥—♥—♥—♥—♥

"IT'S NOT THE DRESS THAT MAKES YOU BEAUTIFUL, RACHEL. IT'S EVERYTHING THAT MAKES UP YOU."

DANYELLE FERGUSON
SWEET CONFECTIONS

♥—♥—♥—♥—♥—♥—♥—♥—♥—♥

CHARACTERS I WOULD DATE

Favorite Fictional Couples

Ship Names for My Favorite Fictional Couples

My Favorite Fictional Break-Ups

Fictional Deaths that Broke My Heart

"There are so many other
sparrows just like me,"
Felicity continued.
"I'm not that special."

At her words, King Taron
leaned forward in his throne.
He studied her, his gaze both
stern and gentle.

"Oh, I must disagree with you,
Mistress Sparrow."
His voice sounded warm
and kind as he spoke. "For no
matter how many sparrows
there are in the world,
there is only one you."

Loralee Evans
Felicity - A Sparrow's Tale

Characters Who Inspired Me

Troubled Characters
Who Fascinated Me

Fictional Characters Who Would Be My Mortal Enemies

BOOKWORM

BOOKWORM

"I am no bird;
and no net ensares me:

I am a free human being
with an independent will."

Charlotte Brontë
Jane Eyre

About the Author

Danyelle Ferguson became a readaholic when she was quite young. As she grew, authors such as Judy Blume and Lurlene McDaniel continued to feed her hunger for more stories. Now she loves discovering new authors and genres (as long as they contain romantic elements). Her favorite book of all time is still Sesame Street's There's a Monster at the End of This Book! Other than reading, she stays busy trying to cram in her writing deadlines between the never-ending laundry pile and constant calls for mom. For more information about Danyelle and her award-winning books, please visit her website - www.DanyelleFerguson.com